W9-BSM-701

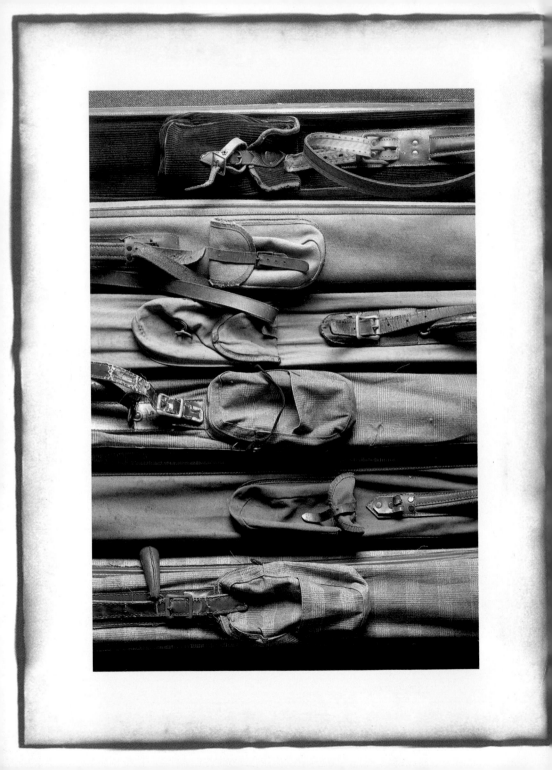

PRESENTED TO

_____

BY

_____

DATE

_____

Project editor: Jenny Baumgartner

Designed by Koechel Peterson, Inc., Minneapolis, Minnesota

Photo credits:

Koechel Peterson & Associates – Cover, Endpapers, 1, 2, 4, 5, 13, 16, 17, 22, 25, 29, 31,
32, 33, 35, 37, 41, 44, 46, 49, 52-53, 56, 61, 63, 64-65, 70, 73, 75, 78, 79, 80, 82, 83, 85,
88, 93, 94, 97, 101, 102-103, 107, 108, 109, 118, 121, 124, 126, 127, 128.

Back Cover, 3, 115 © Macduff Everton/CORBIS; 8, © Rick Parker Photograhy/El Cajon, CA;
10, © TSM/Bod Woodward, 1990; 26, Stan Badz/PGA TOUR; 39, PGA TOUR;
50-51, © Tony Roberts/CORBIS; 62, © Chris Condon/PGA TOUR; 77, © TSM/Torlief
Svensson, 1997; 98, © Stan Badz/PGA TOUR; 104, © Tony Roberts/CORBIS; 105, ©
Bettman/CORBIS; 111, © TSM/R. Steedman, 1985; 116, © Reuters Newmedia Inc/CORBIS;
117, © Reuters Newmedia Inc/CORBIS; 117, © Reuters Newmedia Inc/CORBIS.

ISBN: 0-8499-5526-2

Printed and bound in Belgium

www.jcountryman.com

Finishing THE COURSE

STRATEGIES *for the* BACK NINE *of* YOUR LIFE

Jim Sheard & Wally Armstrong

J. Countryman
Nashville, Tennessee

Contents

Foreword

Finishing the Course is a wonderful metaphor for life. In golf, you want to start out well, and then you want to play consistently throughout the round. You want to focus on each hole and recover from any adversity. As you anticipate finishing the course, each shot and each hole offer a new opportunity to play up to your potential.

My life has provided the opportunities of a successful golf game. I was

able to play golf well early in my life and retire at age thirty-four. While I never gave up my interest and involvement in golf, I also spent the past fifty-three years on my ranch in Texas. I have continued to participate in the game of golf through tournaments and appearances at many events, and I have maintained many wonderful friends through this great game. Most importantly, I have cultivated my faith in God and lived a life consistent with that faith. Peggy and I have found this faith to be our bond in our marriage and in our commitments.

It has been my pleasure to read the tremendous lessons Wally and Jim have provided in this book. They have revealed how we can learn about life and faith by looking closely at the game of golf and have presented valuable biblical insights. I enjoy reading regularly from their first two books, and now I am pleased to be a part of this one. I encourage every golfer to seriously consider these nine strategies so that you can savor "the back nine of your life" as I have.

Finishing the Course will help you think about how you'd like to be remembered and then will encourage you to live the rest of your life that way.

It is a wonderful game, and this is a wonderful life. Enjoy them, and keep the faith.

There is no substitute for experience, and the more you learn to react properly under pressure, the better you'll be able to perform the next time.

Byron Nelson

Introduction

The man who first introduced me to golf was a fellow minister-friend with whom I had gone to school. Whenever we played, he volunteered to keep score, but after a few rounds, it dawned on me that he always got the lowest score in our foursome of pastors.

One day we came to a small lake, and rather than take a penalty and move on if we went into the drink, he challenged us to hit until we got one on the other side. Believe it or not, all three of us hit our first drive safely to the other side, putting enormous pressure on him. It took him seven balls to get across. Later I noticed that he only counted two of those water balls.

One time he had three balls going at the same time and claimed the one with the lowest score was his "official" ball. Other times, instead of counting short putts, he just picked up his ball and said, "That's a gimme." Finally, I got up enough nerve to suggest that his best club was his pencil, which was why he always got the lowest score.

Over time, I have noticed that anyone who cheats in golf has a tendency to cheat in life. My friend was no exception. Of the four of us, this man was decidedly the best preacher, and the most highly respected in his denomination. Yet, the truth is, he

was a cheat! He cheated in golf, and he cheated in life. He cheated on his wife, his church, his Lord, and his family. Today he is a hollow shell of what he could have been.

Life is much like golf; it must be played by the rules. When you cheat, it not only ruins the game, but it also reveals a serious character flaw. And your character defines who you are. Fortunately, with God's help, a weak or poor character can be changed for a lifetime. The apostle Paul, a classic illustration of change, said, "For the message of the cross . . . to us who are being saved it is the power of God" (1 Cor. 1:18). That power is still demonstrated today as thousands of people of weak character are transformed into examples of honor and strength.

Our character is tested every time we play the game of golf; for under the constant pressure to keep our score down, we are tempted to "fudge." It's no sin to be tempted to cheat on the seventeenth hole when no one is watching, but it's our character that determines whether we act on it. And so it is in life.

Jim and Wally are to be commended for this excellent comparison of life and golf, particularly the importance of "the back nine of your life." While it is important to start right, the real test of your character and Christian life is in how you finish. A faithful life means keeping your eye on the goal and applying the strategies presented in this book. While what our peers see in us is important, what really matters is to finish and stand before Jesus Christ, as we will someday, and hear him say, "Well done, good and faithful servant; you have been faithful over a few things, I will make you ruler over many things. Enter into the joy of your lord" (Matt. 25:23).

Col 3: 15-17

Preface

Finishing the Course is about your life. By accepting the sacrifice Jesus made for you, by believing that He has made you perfect in the eyes of God, your own scorecard will not matter. The score for your life will be based on what God has done for you, not your accomplishments. In 1 Corinthians, Paul encourages us to exercise self-control, to seek the imperishable wreath of eternal life with Jesus Christ, rather than perishable trophies of the world. When we serve Jesus, we qualify for the wreath. The only way to finish is by giving yourself to Him in faith, and the nine strategies in this book will

help you do just that. They will strengthen your faith, trust, and confidence for the back nine of your life. They will help you serve God faithfully to the finish.

Each of us will "end" on the eighteenth at St. Andrews, the finishing hole of the birthplace of golf. We will hit our shots and head for the final green and the historic Royal and Ancient clubhouse. As we cross the creek, Jesus will meet us on the Swilcan Bridge and will greet us, one at a time. He will know if you have put your faith in Him. He will recognize those who have finished strong. The back nine will have prepared you so that as He takes your hand, He will say, "Well done, good and faithful servant" (Matt. 25:23).

The following chapters represent the back-nine holes of a golf course. On each hole, you will encounter a strategy, a valuable approach not only for golf, but also for life. The tenth chapter—"The Nineteenth Hole"—offers ideas on how to reflect on what you have learned. Regardless of how you played the front, you can play well on the back. Sound strategies will help you "finish the course."

Life is like golf. Wherever you are, you can finish strong.

JIM SHEARD
WALLY ARMSTRONG
SPRING 2000

Perhaps that's why
I enjoy golf;
it puts in eighteen holes
what life puts in
eighty years—
ups and downs
and a few good bounces.

MAX LUCADO

Vision

VISUALIZE *Your* STRONG *Finish*

I have fought the good fight, I have finished the race, I have kept the faith.
Finally, there is laid up for me the crown of righteousness, which the Lord,
the righteous Judge, will give to me on that Day . . .

2 TIMOTHY 4:7–8

Daily Formula

Fortunately, wherever you are, you still can finish strong. But don't delay in developing your vision. You cannot know how many days, months, or years you have left. You may be young and vibrant one moment, but then tragedy could strike in the blink of an eye.

If you will place your confidence in the one true God, He will forgive your sins and help you see your unique place in the world. Now is the time to put your trust in Him and to begin to visualize a strong finish.

You can make an eternal impact by giving your unique talents, gifts, and resources back to God. God does not expect perfection, just your best. The key is progress, not perfection;

process, not results. A strong finish involves starting, staying, and finishing with Christ every day. God's purposes have more eternal value than any earthly triumph.

God reveals His plan, the vision for your life, as you build a relationship with Christ. You become more like Christ as you learn to communicate with Him and follow His guidance. Approach each day, decision, relationship, and obstacle with growing discernment, seeking to have Paul's perspective in 2 Timothy 4:7–8.

Never give up
on the next shot,
the current round,
or the course of your life.

Our vision is to serve the risen Savior.

PUT FORTH YOUR BEST EFFORT
—fight the good fight—

GO THE DISTANCE
—finish the course—

KEEP THE FAITH
—let Jesus direct your path—

Byron Nelson
A STRONG *Finish*

Byron Nelson kept a notebook between 1935 and 1947. In it, Nelson writes, "While reviewing my notebook records after the 1944 season, I concluded two things: I wasn't concentrating as well as I could, and my chipping wasn't as good as it needed to be . . . With my notebook in hand, I resolved to make 1945 my best year yet. I would focus on the golf course and be more consistently accurate with my chips around the green. . . . The rest, as they say, is history." In 1945, he had a record-setting streak of eleven wins in a row, and he won eighteen of the thirty events he entered.

Byron has demonstrated that by focusing on the right things and becoming more consistent, we can visualize a strong finish. PGA Tour player and U.S. Open Champion Scott Simpson said of Byron, "If I have a hero in golf, he'd be the one.

He's come to our Bible studies and shared just how important his faith is to him. He's said how great everything has worked out in his life, how he has more friends than anybody he's known, and how it is only because he's tried his best to do what the Bible has told him to do. It is that simple. He's had his failures and his successes, but he's always had that goal in mind: to follow the Book! . . . You don't see many guys who are in their eighties with so much joy in their lives."

Byron has been as consistent in life as he was in golf. He has a great sense of balance about life. He invested himself in the right things. He shows us that you are never too young, or too old, to demonstrate your faith by reaching out to people with respect.

Visualize your finish, on and off the course.

Real faith means learning to see beyond the challenges.

A STRONG FINISH REQUIRES . . .
a daily focus on Jesus.

*Y*OU MUST HAVE . . .
the desire to visualize
a strong finish,
the heart to commit
to what you
cannot see,
and the will to
submit
to the
authority
of God.

The Ultimate Game Plan

You must have a game plan to play golf well.

It helps to have a plan not only for the course but also for each shot. Great players picture each shot mentally before executing their swing. They practice for hours and hours, focusing on execution. As they train, their results improve.

Jesus had an ultimate game plan. He executed it through His life.

Jesus' goal is found in John 8:29, in which He explains to His disciples, "I always do those things that please Him." Jesus' focus was on a one-on-one relationship with His Father, rather than on effort, words, or works. He spent time alone with God, meditating, talking, and sharing. That's where Jesus gained His strength.

Our game plan should be the same as Christ's: to live a life pleasing to the Father.

On the course of life, the focus of our game plan must be on the Word of God and the lordship of Jesus Christ. We're to live our lives based on the Scriptures, remembering that Psalm 37:4 says, "Delight yourself also in the Lord, and He shall give you the desires of your heart."

Profile
Harvey Penick
TAKE *Dead* AIM

For sixty years, Harvey Penick was a golf teacher and philosopher on life. Today, he is revered by the many amateur and professional golfers who were his students. He is known for his impact on famous golfers like Tom Kite, Ben Crenshaw, Davis Love Jr., Kathy Whitworth, Mickey Wright, and Betsy Rawls. His watchful eye and gentle wisdom helped members of his club and others who traveled great distances to learn from him.

Many have become disciples of his wisdom through the ideas he recorded in his *Little Red Book*. One of his ideas is "Take Dead Aim!" In golf, it means to focus your swing on the target. But it can also apply to life: focusing your attention on your goals each day, week, month, and year. It suggests the need for a vision, one that aims for the finish of your life and takes *dead aim*, each day, on that strong finish with Christ. Harvey's strong faith in Christ helped him reach people. He humbled himself, gave to others, and avoided earthly glory so that others might become all that God intended them to be.

Those who knew Harvey often talk about the impact he made on those around him. For example, Ben Crenshaw delayed his preparation for the 1995 Masters so that he could visit Harvey on his deathbed in Texas. Even then, Harvey gave Ben advice on his putting stroke. Ben was a pallbearer at Harvey's funeral; he then returned to Augusta, intent on playing the Masters as a tribute to his master teacher. Ben won, giving cred-it to Harvey in an emotional victory on the eighteenth green.

Jesus is our foremost teacher, and we are His disciples. Our lives should reflect His teachings. He wants us to take His message to others, to show them what He has written, and to tell them what He means to us. Take dead aim on your finish with Jesus.

Live each day as a tribute to your Master!

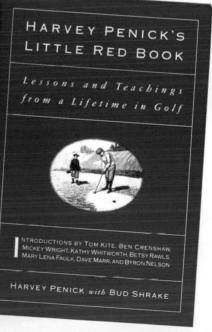

HARVEY PENICK'S
LITTLE RED BOOK

Lessons and Teachings from a Lifetime in Golf

INTRODUCTIONS BY TOM KITE, BEN CRENSHAW, MICKEY WRIGHT, KATHY WHITWORTH, BETSY RAWLS, MARY LENA FAULK, DAVE MARR, AND BYRON NELSON

HARVEY PENICK *with* BUD SHRAKE

The Right *Stuff*

Richard Carlson's recent book, *Don't Sweat the Small Stuff . . . and it's all small stuff*, describes our tendency to get worked up over little details that are unimportant. Many golfers are guilty of this habit. They think about far too many things during their golf swing, complicating it way out of proportion. But there are some important things a golfer should consider—the "right stuff" to practice for the course.

- GET A GRIP—You cannot play without a proper grip; it is the foundation of the golf swing just as God's grip is the foundation for your life.

- ALIGN WITH THE TARGET— If you do not know where you are heading, you'll end up where you don't want to be. Align your club face, feet, and shoulders with the target.

- USE THE POWER OF CENTRIFUGAL FORCE—The power of the golf swing comes from centrifugal force. This force is created by the arc of the club head as it follows a flat plane — from the take away, to the top, through the ball, and to the finish.

- SEE IT, FEEL IT, AND TRUST IT— Sports psychologist Dr. David L. Cook says, "See the shot in your mind, feel it happen in your body, and then trust your ability to make it happen . . . accept the consequences."

Practice the "right stuff,"
and the rest
will become "small stuff."

"Start from the Finish" DRILL

Ben Hogan said the swing should be thought of as one complete motion, even though the club head moves approximately twenty-seven feet from its starting position behind the ball to the top of the finish. You can practice this motion with this "start from the finish" drill.

First practice without a ball. The drill begins by placing the club head just behind a tee. Take the club forward—over the top of the tee—all the way to the finish of your swing. From there, slowly take the club back, past the setup position to the top of your backswing. From there, begin your normal swing through to the top of your finish. Go slowly, feeling the entire swing, just clipping the top of the tee. Gradually increase the tempo to your normal swing speed. Then, repeat the drill with a ball on the tee, but do not focus on the ball. Instead, emphasize the total flowing motion. You will be amazed how long and straight the ball will go with a smooth, easy swing.

Now, in a similar fashion, focus on the finish of your life. What do you want your finish to look like? Be optimistic but realistic. Do not get hung up on the unimportant details of life that distract from your focus. When you start with the finish—that is, look to heaven and the Father—the things of this world will begin to fall into place.

*Visualize the path of your life.
Begin with where
you are now, and end
with a strong finish
with the Father in heaven.*

PLAYING *Your* BACK NINE

*"And He who sent Me is with Me. The Father has not left Me alone,
for I always do those things that please Him."*

JOHN 8:29

In the back nine of life, we often change our goals and redefine our vision. As you visualize your own strategy for a strong finish, consider these questions:

- *Where does the Lord want me at this time?*

- *How does He want to refine my character to serve Him and His people?*

- *How can I be a better spouse, parent, grandparent?*

- *How can I invest my time to the greatest advantage for God's kingdom?*

- *What has God uniquely prepared me to do for Him at this time in my life?*

In his late thirties, Jim wrote two to four life goals in several categories, including spiritual, family, career, and financial. Other than updating the specifics, these goals were relevant until his midfifties. Looking back, however, they were mainly front-nine goals. At fifty-five years of age, Jim made the turn to the back nine of his life. Most of his financial and career goals had been met with the grace of God, but he refined his vision of the finish. He "retired" to become an author of books on golf and life. His goals for the back nine focus on making an impact for Christ in ways for which God has prepared him. As an encourager, speaker, and writer, he strives to be sensitive to the Lord's leading.

**Vision is seeing the plan.
Execution is doing it.**

STRATEGY TWO
Commitment
WALK *with the* MASTER

Jesus said to him, "I am the way, the truth, and the life.
No one comes to the Father except through Me."

JOHN 14:6

In the 1970s, a presentation at a PGA Tour chapel focused on Ecclesiastes 9:3b–4, "Truly the hearts of the sons of men are full of evil . . . But for him who is joined to all the living there is hope, for a living dog is better than a dead lion."

The speaker explained that there are many lion carcasses lying around—those of men and women who have built their lives on the wrong foundations. Oh, their manes may look good and their presentations may sound great, but, in the end, they are dead lions. They've lived for happiness instead of joy and sought prosperity instead of posterity.

By contrast, to be fully alive, we must walk with the Master down the fairways of life. This second strategy for the back nine of your life involves making Christ your foundation. By committing to a relationship with Jesus, and by learning from God's Word, you will become increasingly like Him.

What is the basis for your life? Are you a dead lion or a live dog? Do you have a good appearance on the outside but are lost on the inside? The key is knowing for whom and for what you stand. In 2 Timothy 4:8, Paul says that the prize for those who are alive in Christ will be the "crown of righteousness."

Jesus is the answer.
He is worthy
of your commitment.

Jesus' greatest work was not His miracles,

but His time spent alone with His Father.

RUSSELL KELFER

Bernhard Langer
EASTER *is the* MASTER'S DAY

Bernhard Langer walks with the Master. He tells people in his native Germany, and throughout the world, the testimony of how God became real to him. He explains, "I thought I had everything: money, victory, fame, and a wonderful family. But something was missing." He was the leading player in the world, having won tournaments across the globe, and then in 1985, he won his first Masters. Then, during the 1985 Heritage Classic in Charleston, Bernhard and his wife Vikki were invited by Bobby Clampett to the LINKS Fellowship Bible study on the Tour. Bernhard won that tournament, but more importantly, as a result of what he learned at the study, Bernhard committed his life to Jesus Christ. He says, "God replaced my reliance on winning and on things with the peace of God's love." The real Master came into Bernhard's life; Jesus was that missing part.

Bernhard later won the Masters a second time in 1993. This win came on Easter Sunday, and in an interview in the Butler cabin, he told the television audience how grateful he was to have won the tournament for the second time on Easter. He expressed his faith by explaining that Easter is the day on which his Lord was resurrected to give new life to all those who will believe in Him. His focus in 1993 was far different than in 1985. Bernhard was a new person in Christ.

Bernhard is respected for continually sharing his faith journey with thousands around the world. Many have come to walk with the real Master after hearing Bernhard explain how Christ became real in his life. Walking with the Savior will not assure anyone of winning the Masters or any other golf event, but it will give new meaning to life. It will place your victories and defeats in the proper perspective.

Walking with the Master means that every day is Easter.

Character *for the* Course

*Forgetting those things which are behind and reaching forward
to those things which are ahead, I press toward the goal
for the prize of the upward call of God in Christ Jesus.*

PHILIPPIANS 3:13–14

Golf is a character-revealing, if not a character-building, game. In the final analysis, character is more important than how well we play the game. We often focus our attention on our successes, our accomplishments, our gains—including the car we drive or the house we live in—and on whether we win or lose. We often seek titles, a higher income, and the next promotion. But what God cares about is our character. He uses challenges, or even difficult golf holes, to help develop our character.

Golf refines our character because we are unable to control or perfect our game. If we could achieve total control, then there would be no character building. Life is the same way. Because we cannot control the circumstances and outcomes, our character grows, and we learn to trust God.

Adversity can help bring our character into conformity with God. With the right perspective, adverse experiences help refine our character into His likeness.

The ultimate aim of golf lies not in victory or defeat, but in the perfection of the character of the participants.

The ultimate aim of life lies not in our accomplishments or success, but in the perfection of our character in the likeness of Christ.

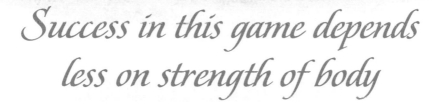

Success in this game depends less on strength of body

than strength of mind and character.

ARNOLD PALMER

Jerry Achenbach
A MAN *of* PURPOSE

Jerry Achenbach was successful in business as the CEO of Piggly Wiggly Southern, a food chain headquartered in southern Georgia. He served as president and chairman of the board for thirty-three years prior to his retirement in 1975. In golf, he had opportunities most of us only dream about. He was a member not only of Augusta National but also of the Royal and Ancient Golf Club of St. Andrews. He also belonged to the Capital City Golf Club in Atlanta and Vidalia Country Club in Vidalia, Georgia.

His personal life, too, was successful. He lived on a beautiful farm with his six adopted children and had eleven grandchildren. His home for children in Vidalia, Georgia, was run by world-class weight lifter Paul Anderson, a mighty Christian who was known as the world's strongest man.

Jerry knew his purpose in life was unrelated to all those successes. In August 1987, he said his personal goal was "to concentrate on living my life in such a way that my every thought and action are in accordance with God's will and acceptable in His sight, to the end that I am ready at any time to depart into the next world with no sense of remorse." When he died on October 20, 1996, Jerry had achieved his goal; he had served God in many ways.

His interest in golf and his great faith sparked his commitment to combine the two. He was an early founder of LINKS Fellowship and College Golf Fellowship. He was described by Tom Flory, a friend and fellow encourager of these ventures, as "a man of vision, [with] a thirst for the truth and the capacity to share it with others. Those who knew him were enriched by his friendship.

We all miss the vitality with which he flavored our lives, and yet, at the same time, we celebrate and rejoice with him because he is now at home with Jesus."

Be committed to
a worthwhile purpose
that serves
Jesus Christ!

DAILY COMMITMENT TO JESUS

is walking hand-in-hand

WITH THE

MASTER!

Commitment *Means* Time

But we know that when He is revealed, we shall be like Him,
for we shall see Him as He is. And everyone who has this
hope in Him purifies himself, just as He is pure.

1 JOHN 3:2b–3

Our goal, as people of faith, is to live so that our character becomes like that of Christ. Having the character of Christ is not a list of dos and don'ts. Nor is it based on what you are able to do for Him. It cannot be bought or earned; it is given by Him. It comes from "being in Christ," not from "doing for Christ."

The Scriptures show that whenever Jesus was in a difficult situation, He went to a quiet place to be with His Father. When His heart was filled with His Father's presence and will, He returned to fulfill His responsibilities. Thus, the work He accomplished while on earth was not His own; He was doing the work of His Father.

Jesus came to reveal His Father to us; our only real accomplishments come from total faith in Jesus.

Acquiring the character of the Master comes from a relationship with the Lord Jesus Christ.

Finding *the* Solution

He heals the brokenhearted and binds up their wounds.

PSALM 147:3

In a 1997 interview with David Frost, Dr. Billy Graham identified four problems of the human spirit: emptiness, loneliness, guilt, and fear of death. Dr. Graham has traveled the world for several decades sharing the only real solution to these problems: Jesus Christ. He has preached to millions, including several times at Bible studies on the PGA Tour, telling the good news of the gospel.

Jesus' death on the cross and His resurrection from the dead fills the void. However, people search in all the wrong places, trying to fill the void with food, sex, drugs, alcohol, and medicines and therapies. They join groups, take classes, and read books and articles. While these may provide temporary relief, only Jesus fills the vacuum.

This search for wholeness is a bit like repairing a broken-down golf swing. Golfers look everywhere for a solution. We become convinced that our swing can be fixed with a new driver, fairway wood, putter, or a classy wedge. We buy some gimmick or training aid. We look for solutions in infomercials, golf stores, golf magazines, and catalogues. But we overlook what really needs to be fixed . . . ourselves.

A competent teaching professional can diagnose the problem and coach us into a better swing, standing by to give any further instruction. Jesus is like that. He is available by invitation to come into your life, repair the pain, and stick by you for corrections.

Jesus fills the God-sized void in your spirit.

CHOOSE *to* WALK *with the* MASTER

He who says he abides in Him
ought himself also to walk just as He walked.

1 JOHN 2:6

Though golf is a game of rules, we may choose to stretch them or to make up our own. In finishing the course of life, we face similar temptations, but the looseness in our society's moral values can be countered by the Bible's absolutes. On the back nine of your life, your basic "rules" should focus on the following principles.

CHOOSE TO BELIEVE . . .

- The Bible presents God's truth about life.
- God created man and earth.
- Jesus died on the cross and paid the penalty for my sins.
- Therefore, by faith in Him, we will be united with God eternally.

WALK WITH JESUS . . .

- Live your life according to biblical principles. Read and learn from the Bible regularly.
- Fellowship with, and learn from, godly men and women.
- Pray to God regularly. Give Him praise and honor. Ask for His help.
- Abide in Jesus by patterning your life and character after Him.

Identity

KNOW *Your* PURPOSE

For we are His workmanship, created in Christ Jesus for good works,
which God prepared beforehand that we should walk in them.

EPHESIANS 2:10

You may feel that you are moving along the course of life not knowing where you are headed. Does it feel like you are just along for the ride? Do you ever ask, "Why am I here? What am I doing?" The good news is that God has created you for a reason, to know and serve Him. He wants you to acknowledge Him as Lord, to be "in His grip." Moreover, He gave you unique capabilities and experiences, and He wants to use them for His kingdom.

Knowing your identity will reveal your purpose. God can help us understand how to utilize our talents, experiences, and gifts to serve Him. We are never too young or old to learn from the experiences and resources God provides. However, as we grow older, the question "Why am I here?" takes on greater significance. Insights from the front nine of life can help you recognize how to serve Him on the back nine. In golf, we each have different skills and backgrounds and must, therefore, approach the course in different ways to play well and enjoy ourselves.

> *God has created you*
> *for a purpose,*
> *to know*
> *and serve Him.*

*I've always believed
that golfers need to know
their own game,*

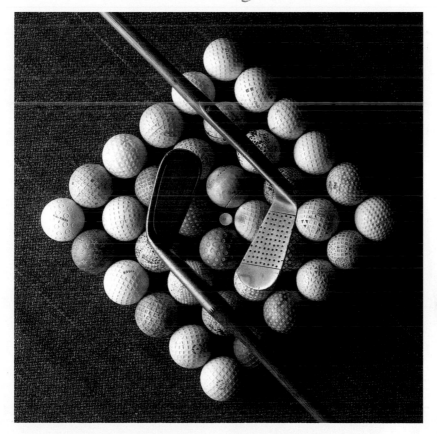

*what they're capable of and
what they're not.*

TOM LEHMAN

Rik Massengale
MY IDENTITY *is in* CHRIST

Golf became an integral part of Rik Massengale's life at age twelve. His brother Don was on the PGA Tour, and Rik's ability cemented his desire to play in college and become a pro. While at the University of Texas, Rik remembers, "Because achieving at golf was so important to me, everything else in my life was affected by the way I played. . . . My identity was totally tied up in being a golfer. I was fine as long as I was around golfers and people who knew of my golfing abilities. But if I was around people who didn't know of my achievements, I became very insecure."

Rik qualified for the PGA Tour in 1970, but by his fourth year, his self-worth was at an all-time low. He wasn't playing well, and his marriage was in trouble to the point of preparing for a divorce. One Sunday, while flipping television channels, he and his wife Cindy came across a movie about the life of Jesus, *The Greatest Story Ever Told*, and realized they were missing something. A short time later, at the Tour Bible study in Charlotte in June of 1974, they heard Billy Graham describe Christianity as a personal relationship with Jesus Christ. Soon after, they received Jesus into their lives. Over time, he says, "My wife and I started seeing our relationship growing closer, only because our main priority was getting to know Christ better by reading the Scriptures together and praying together. As we started growing closer to God, we started seeing that our marriage and our relationship as a couple were improving."

Rik's greatest success on Tour came in the mid-70s when he won three tournaments, including the prestigious Bob Hope Desert Classic in 1977. By then his identity was no longer in golf; it was in God. In recent years, as the director of College Golf Fellowship, he has been sharing the gospel of Jesus Christ with college golfers and coaches. Rik is helping many others find their purpose, or as he calls it, "Discover Why You're Here!"

Discover your identity in Christ.

Seek WISDOM

And Solomon said: . . . "Therefore give to Your servant an understanding heart to judge Your people, that I may discern between good and evil."

1 KINGS 3:9

The Lord appeared to Solomon in a dream and said, "Ask! What shall I give you?" (1 Kings 3:5). Solomon praised God, thanked Him for His kindness to his father David, admitted his inadequacy, and asked to be God's servant. He asked for wisdom in fulfilling the duties God had given him because he wanted to have the heart and mind to do God's will, not his own. Solomon's response revealed five areas of his heart. Solomon knew:

What to ask for—He wanted what God wanted.

His place—He was God's servant as the king.

His dependence—He knew he could not do it himself.

His competence—God's there when you're over your head.

His sphere of influence—His potential was in God.

God granted Solomon's wish for wisdom and discernment and even bestowed gifts upon Solomon that he did not ask for—wealth, honor, and long life.

God is asking you, "What do you want?" Your response reveals your heart. Do you know what to ask for? Do you know your place, dependence, competence, and sphere of influence? Ask God for wisdom and discernment. Give back what is His. He will give you even more.

God issues a request, asking what you want from Him. Your response reveals your heart and your motives. He will reward what you ask for and note what you omit.

Ask God how you can best serve Him.

MY PURPOSE IN LIFE
IS TO *know God* AND TO
pursue Him AT ANY COST.

WALLY ARMSTRONG

Peggy Kirk Bell
The LEGEND

In May 1999, *Golf* magazine called her "Living Legend No. 1 in women's golf—the indomitable, lovable Peggy Kirk Bell." Though *Webster's* defines

indomitable as "unyielding, unconquerable," the love of Jesus conquered Peggy and created her identity in Christ. Her faith shaped her commitment to others, which made her so lovable. As a seventeen-year-old girl growing up in Findlay, Ohio, in 1939, Peggy became intrigued by golf. She tried it one day—all day—then took her first lesson the next day. She continued to take lessons, practiced incessantly, and even as a teenager, became indomitable. Peggy was a three-time winner of the Ohio Women's Amateur Championship, won the International Four Ball Championship with Babe Zaharias in 1947, and won the Pinehurst North and South Amateur and Augusta

Titleholders Championships in 1949. In 1950, she was on the Curtis Cup team, won the Eastern Amateur Championship, and published *A Woman's Way to Better Golf*. As a pro, she represented A. G. Spalding and was inducted into the North Carolina Hall of Fame.

In 1953, Peggy and her husband Warren purchased the Pine Needles golf resort between Pinehurst and Southern Pines, North Carolina. There, in the heart of one of the world's great golf centers, the couple was devoted to their family, golf, and God. When cancer took Warren's life, Peggy courageously forged ahead, finding time to give to others. She hosted the first Fellowship of Christian Athletes Youth Golf Camp twenty years ago and has hosted a camp every year since. Her family purchased Mid Pines Inn and Golf Club in 1994, and they now operate these adjacent Donald Ross golf

resorts. When asked how this all came about, Peggy said, "I think the Lord just directed my life."

When your identity is in Christ, He directs your life. He helps you to know your real purpose.

Know *Your* Game

Every golfer scores better
when he learns his capabilities.

TOMMY ARMOUR

To finish strong, you should know your capabilities and appreciate the unique way God has created and gifted you. You also need insight and should openly accept feedback from others. "SHAPE" is one good way to understand your identity in Christ. Created by Saddleback Valley Community Church in Mission Viejo, California, SHAPE is an acronym of five categories of information.

God wants to utilize your unique SHAPE for His kingdom.

S — *Spiritual Gifts*
H — *Heart, Passions*
A — *Abilities*
P — *Personality*
E — *Experience, "Know How"*

You need to identify the good and bad parts of your game as well as the shots that are within your capabilities. Jim learned this on a par four over a river at his home course. He could not carry the water if he aimed for the middle of the fairway. Even though the hole had a dogleg right, he had to play safely to the left in order to clear the water. From there, he could get his second shot in front of the elevated green with a chance to chip and putt for par.

Focus *for* Life

Jesus said to him, "I am the way, the truth, and the life.
No one comes to the Father except through Me.
If you had known Me, you would have known my Father also;
and from now on, you know Him and have seen Him."

JOHN 14:6–7

We need a focus for our life. We need to avoid the distractions. By committing ourselves to Jesus, we have God's Spirit living in us to guide and encourage our thoughts and actions. He helps us see the image of what we are to do each step of the way. As we play each shot in life, He encourages and helps correct our action. God's Word teaches us principles that focus our attention and help make the path smooth. He shows us the way out of difficulties by teaching us to trust His guidance.

Let Jesus
be the focus
of your life!

Wally played some of his best golf on the PGA Tour when his former college roommate, Joe, caddied for him. They coordinated a routine that provided focus for each hole and each shot. First, they determined the worst that could happen considering the out-of-bounds stakes, the wind direction and velocity, and hazards. Next, Joe pushed Wally to focus on the best shot based on his abilities and confidence level. After they agreed on the club, Joe gave it to Wally and said, "Okay, practice that swing exactly as you are going to hit the shot." Wally then took a practice swing, conceptualizing the swing motion and flight of the ball. Joe also encouraged Wally by saying, "Okay, play the shot Wally. You can do it!" This helped Wally to trust the picture and have confidence in the shot as planned. The routine encouraged a simple, positive movement without hesitation or blocking out.

Maximize Your Greatest Assets

Look for your own best assets
and try to find a way
to play that maximizes them.

JACK NICKLAUS
GOLF MY WAY

IDENTITY *with* PURPOSE

*These things I have written to you who believe in the name of
the Son of God, that you may know that you have eternal life, . . .
Now this is the confidence that we have in Him,
that if we ask anything according to His will, He hears us.*

1 JOHN 5:13–14

Life would be futile if we simply existed for a period of time, died, and turned back to dust. However, God created the universe and you with a purpose. Discovering God's purpose for your life is a lifelong process of growing in faith in God, learning about Him and His will for your life, and discovering His resources for you. When Bob Buford walked this path of discovery, he said, "I knew what I believed, but I didn't really know what I planned to do about what I believed." God will help you discover your "identity with a purpose" as you answer the following questions.

- How can I read His Word, listen for His voice, watch for His direction, and take steps that will show me His path for my life?

- What can God use for His glory from my experiences, abilities, spiritual gifts, interests, passions, and sphere of influence?

- What purpose or mission for my life will have the greatest impact for Him?

- What is God's vision for my life? Why has He created me at this time and place?

- What eternal legacy can I leave in my family, community, work, and church?

You are called to a purpose, not driven toward a goal.

Relationships

PICK *Your* FOURSOME

Now may the God of patience and comfort grant you to be likeminded toward one another, according to Christ Jesus . . .

ROMANS 15:5

Selecting and spending time with the right people enhances your growth and theirs, but your most important relationship is with Christ. Make it number one. The second most important relationship is with your spouse, and your children are your next priority. Raise them to honor God and serve Him. Nothing will have greater value to them. Parents, in-laws, and other relatives are also important relationships.

Your closest nonfamily relationships should include individuals who hold you accountable in your life and faith. You may meet with them in a Bible study or accountability group. These relationships exist "to prepare God's people for works of service, so that the body of Christ may be built up until we all reach unity in the faith and in the knowledge of the Son of God and become mature, attaining to the whole measure of the fullness of Christ" (Eph. 4:12–13, NIV). These are the individuals for whom you would drop everything to help in times of trouble and with whom you can rejoice during the good times. They are special people provided by God. Spend time with them, and build a bond. They are "your foursome" for the course of life.

You can experience great fellowship on the course. If you are selective about who is in your regular golf foursome, it can be an opportunity to encourage one another in golf and life. Be open to what God is doing within your group.

Allow God to be a part of your round.

Our jobs are not as important

as our faith, our family, and our friends.

BOB ESTES

At the 1999 Tour Championship following Payne Stewart's death

Bill Rogers
The RIGHT PLACE *and* PEOPLE

Bill Rogers' biggest success in golf was winning the British Open at the Royal St. Georges Golf Club and being named PGA Player of the Year in 1981. He had already won three other tournaments that year, and he went on to win two in Japan, two in Australia, and two in the United States (the World Series of Golf and the Texas Open).

Along the way, God had been at work in Bill's life. Rik Massengale and Larry Nelson invited him to the Tour Bible study. Though he had accepted Jesus Christ into his life as his Lord and Savior in 1976, Bill says, "Golf was still truly my god. I did not fully understand my commitment to follow Christ. I was still committed to following the lure of the almighty dollar and the success at any price. I was playing the game for the wrong reasons."

But God had a different plan for Bill's life, one that would shift his desires from worldly success to those that honored God and His kingdom. As Bill's competitive edge and skills began to slip, God was molding and shaping Bill's character. Bill eventually left the Tour to become director of golf at San Antonio Country Club. Today, Bill strives to honor God in all that he does.

Bill ended up in the right place and devoted to the right people. He is a successful club professional and a devoted family man. The high priority of his family is evident in the number of family photos on his desk and credenza. By contrast, his office contains little evidence of his incredible success on the PGA Tour. His life motto is adapted from Luke's gospel, "To whom much is given, to whom much is entrusted, much is required."

Let God shape your priorities.

To follow Christ as you walk the fairways and greens is no easy task. These golfers [on the tours] are faced with temptations and challenges few of us realize, but they will tell you that there is no person they would rather have in their foursome than the Nazarene carpenter. He may not keep every ball in play, but he does keep every soul in his hand. And so you don't have to be a scratch golfer to be on his team.

MAX LUCADO

Jim Hiskey
PICKING *a* FOURSOME

Jim Hiskey grew up in Idaho where he was the Idaho State Amateur Champion three times. He then chose to play at the University of Houston where he was an All-American; his team won the NCAA Championship three years in a row. After college, he wavered between becoming a campus minister or a professional golfer, but he chose to play professional golf and soon became an expert player and instructor. He won over thirty professional and amateur events and instructed members of congress and heads of state.

He has fulfilled a bigger dream by serving golfers throughout the world as an ambassador for the Lord. Jim, his brother Babe, Kermit Zarley, Wally Armstrong, and others started the Bible study on the PGA Tour. Billy Graham and others taught the pros, and eventually, Larry Moody became the regular study leader. As it grew, the golfers on the Tour reached out to amateur golfers, and it came to be known as the LINKS Ministry, which Jim headed for many years. Its newsletter, *The LINKS Letter*, reached sixty thousand people, and LINKS events and seminars influenced many others.

Jim also led groups of American golfers to other countries, such as Japan, China, and South Africa, where they shared their faith and love of golf. In some cases, following their visit, golfing ministries were established in that country. After leaving the PGA Tour, Jim became a successful PING sales representative in Virginia. His ambassadorship for the Lord has been worldwide and ongoing. Throughout the world, there are people who know and appreciate what Jim Hiskey has done for the game of golf and God's kingdom.

We are ambassadors for the Lord here on earth.

LINKS Players

Jim Hiskey's relationship with Jesus Christ and his love of golf have given him a desire to connect or link golfers, urging them to discover and grow in a one-on-one relationship with God and each other. The LINKS acrostic tells this message:

Love God
with heart, soul, and mind;
and your neighbor as yourself.
(MATT. 22:37–39)

Integrate Christ's Reign
into life, family, and vocation.
(MATT. 6:33)

Network Friends
together in Christ.
(ACTS 2:42)

Kindle Compassionate Concern
for the poor and needy.
(MATT. 25:40)

Share Christ
through the great game of golf.
(2 COR. 5:20A)

Your FOURSOME

Then Daniel went to his house, and made the decision known to Hananiah, Mishael, and Azariah, his companions, that they might seek mercies from the God of heaven concerning this secret, so that Daniel and his companions might not perish with the rest of the wise men of Babylon.

DANIEL 2:17–18

For many people, playing golf is an opportunity to build relationships. Their regular foursome includes their most trusted friends from whom they ask advice on how to improve their game. They also encourage one another in life. The right mix of golfing skills and personalities provides a unique opportunity to learn from one another. One player may have a swing with a very smooth tempo, which others then gradually adopt. Another may be good at encouraging, even if it's just by noting the improvements in the others' swings.

One of the Bible's "foursomes" is David and his close friends. These companions faced execution if they failed to describe and interpret the king's dream. Daniel immediately asked his three godly friends to pray.

What would you have done? Who would you contact for help in a difficult situation? Like Daniel, we need friends to pray with and for us. We need people who are willing to correct us when we are wrong and to pray for us regularly. We need to encourage one another and hold each other accountable for priorities in our faith. Who can you count on to pray for you? Who holds you accountable in your life and faith?

Be on the lookout for the right people to fill your foursome.

Family *Is* First Priority

Husbands, love your wives, just as Christ
also loved the church and gave Himself for her . . .

EPHESIANS 5:25

He will go before Him in the spirit and power of Elijah,
'to turn the hearts of the fathers to the children' . . .

LUKE 1:17

What is getting in the way of the important time you should be spending with your family and God? Are you attracted to something that keeps you from your priorities? Do you spend too much time at golf, work, or some other activity? The good news is that it's not too late for a strong finish. Let God help you make your family a high priority.

Are you
positioned
to finish
strong
with your
family?

Jim was once addicted to finding a good golf swing. He was determined to discover that allusive groove. He played as often as he could, hit balls nearly everyday, and always warmed up before playing. When it worked, it felt good. In a tournament, the sensation was even better. In retrospect, Jim knows, at times, he played golf when he should have been spending time with his wife and twin sons.

Though Jim didn't lose his family, for many others, spending too much time at work, recreation, or even church can leave a gaping hole in their family relationships. Some of their marriages end in divorce. Others lose their children to drugs, sex, or violence. Even when the results are not so obvious, there are subtle losses that cannot be recovered.

ENCOURAGEMENT
for Your
RELATIONSHIPS

THE PRICELESS HERITAGE

To finish strong means that you are leaving your children and grandchildren the priceless heritage of a godly life.

STEVE FARRAR, AUTHOR

SUCCESS AT THE OFFICE

No amount of success at the office can make up for failure at home.

PAT MORLEY, AUTHOR

FAITHFUL WHEREVER YOU ARE

God hasn't called everybody to be working on the PGA Tour. Wherever he puts you, just be faithful.

STEVE JONES,
PGA TOUR GOLFER

THE EVIDENCE OF CHRIST

*The overwhelming evidence of Christ
in other people's lives has shown me
the living evidence of God and Jesus Christ.*

JIM KEMPER,
CHAIRMAN OF THE BOARD, KEMPER INSURANCE GROUP

Perspective

PLAY ONE SHOT at a TIME

Oh, give thanks to the Lord, for He is good!
For His mercy endures forever.

PSALM 107:1

Our best results come when we focus on playing one shot at a time. Do not condemn yourself for prior mistakes, focus too much on your successes, or look too far ahead of yourself. Enjoy each shot, and do your best. That is all you can expect of yourself. Determine the shot you want to play, and then play it.

By focusing on the present, we become more aware of God's work. There is wonder to behold in each person, each creation of God. He gave us a mind, body, and will, and they work together to execute the golf swing. Our memory allows us to relive our experiences and learn from them. But even more spectacular is that we are created in the image of the God who created the universe. In His infinite wisdom, He gave us the capacity to communicate with Him.

Enjoy life one step at a time. Do not miss the wonder of it all, even for a moment. Take time to see beauty on the golf course. Look for His handiwork in nature and in the way He created you. Allow yourself to be in awe of Him. Have an "attitude of gratitude" toward God as He guides you each step of the way to a strong finish on your back nine.

To finish strong,
you must play
one shot at a time.

*Have a
receptive perspective*

*for what God is doing
in your midst.*

Tommy Bolt
DAY-*by*-DAY

Though he was already thirty-four years old when he made it to the Tour, Tommy Bolt became a renowned player in the '50s and '60s. Known as "Thunder," he garnered quite a reputation in the press, and he managed to live up to most of it. This former carpenter admits to hustling, gambling, cussing, and club throwing in the early days.

After his first couple of wins, Tommy was on his way. His achievements included winning the U.S. Open in 1958 (then called the National Open Championship) and fourteen other PGA Tour events throughout his career. Gary Player praised his game, saying, "He had one of the best swings I ever saw."

Now Tommy and Mary Lou, his wife of forty-two years, live and learn one day at a time. Each morning, he devotes time to God's Word and prayer. He has learned that growing in the Lord is a day-by-day process, and he has a reputation as a

man who walks closely with the Master. And he still plays par golf.

What happened to Tommy is evidence of the grace of God. Along the way, Tommy saw his need for the Savior—someone who would accept him as he was and forgive him for his sins. Jesus holds Tommy's hand in a relationship that takes one step at a time, one shot at a time. Tommy didn't change overnight; instead, it was a steady process of growth in character as he walked with the Master. God shows us that the most important shots are the ones we are playing right now. What we do with our life day-by-day is what matters to the Lord. He takes our hand and shows us His way as we walk with Him. Tommy has found that life and faith are simpler when you live day-by-day and trust in the Lord. Have you?

To me the golf swing is simple. People sure make it hard, don't they? But it is a simple thing.

TOMMY BOLT

Tempo *and* Faith

Tommy Bolt tells a story about Dr. Billy Graham to illustrate the relationship between tempo and faith. "I once heard Billy Graham preaching," he begins. "In talking about faith in the good Lord, Billy compared it to driving along an expressway." Dr. Graham described what happens when you travel down an expressway at fifty-five miles per hour and approach the crest of a hill; he said, "You continue along at fifty-five with faith in the road department that there is [a road ahead of you]."

Tommy says, "Blushing a bit, I confess that when I heard this, I compared it to the golf swing. To the downswing of a golf club. I can't tell how many people I've seen swing who do not have faith in what they are doing. . . . I have this faith.

I maintain it because I practice it many hours."

You need to spend time practicing your golf swing so that you have faith in it. And so it is in life: you need a nice, easy tempo. It is important to communicate regularly with God in prayer, to practice the discipline of being in His Word, and to ask Him to speak to us through His Spirit. Like the tempo of your golf swing, your faith improves with practice. It gives you God's perspective.

If you move through your early golfing life with a good tempo, then you will be able to play pretty decent golf all your life.

TOMMY BOLT

See *the Beauty Around* You

The earth is the Lord's, and all its fullness,
the world and those who dwell therein.
For He has founded it upon the seas,
and established it upon the waters.

PSALM 24:1–2

O beautiful for spacious skies, For amber waves of grain, For purple mountain majesties above the fruited plain. America! America! God shed his grace on thee, And crown thy good with brotherhood, From sea to shining sea.

"AMERICA THE BEAUTIFUL"
TEXT BY KATHARINE LEE BATES

In the mind of a golfer, Psalm 24 and the song "America the Beautiful" invoke striking images of golf courses in the mountains of Colorado, Wyoming, or Montana; on the plains of Kansas, Nebraska, Texas, or Oklahoma; and along the scenic east and west coasts. You may recall the sun rising through the trees or setting over the horizon, as found in Psalm 50:1. Or you may recall the beautiful blending of nature and man on a famous or favorite golf course. This is the work of God; the fairways, traps, and greens are the work of a skilled course designer. The most vivid images are those you take time to notice and appreciate.

- *Go to the course to . . .*
- *See God's creation!*
- *Capture a memory!*
- *Thank Him! Worship Him!*

Allow His peace
to rule
in your heart!

THE WINNING PERSPECTIVE IN GOLF AND LIFE

Stay mentally positive.

See yourself winning.

Play one shot at a time.

Focus your mind on the target.

Enjoy the routine, rhythm, and result of each shot.

You will win the old fashioned way: one shot at a time.

$\mathcal{T}$HE MIND
messes up

more shots

THAN THE
BODY.

TOMMY BOLT

"It's History!"

Forgetting those things which are behind and reaching forward to those things which are ahead, I press on toward the goal for the prize of the upward call of God in Christ Jesus.

PHILIPPIANS 3:13b–14

For several years, Wally let disappointments and emotions get in the way of a good game. In his first year on the PGA Tour, he held the lead at the Doral Open. He faced great pressure being paired with Jack Nicklaus and Lee Trevino in the last group on Saturday. Jack took the lead on the thirteenth hole and moved out way ahead of the field. Wally recalls, "On hole sixteen, I hit a beautiful wedge shot about eight feet from the front of the hole. Jack was on the same line, about ten feet beyond the hole, and missed to the left. I blew it to the same side even though I knew exactly how it would break. I could hardly stand it anymore." After slicing the next tee shot into the trap, Wally was walking down the fairway, muttering to himself. Then Lee Trevino put his arm around Wally's neck and said, "Hey, son, forget it. It's history. You can't take that shot back."

"From that point on, I tried to not worry about things I couldn't control," Wally said. "If I missed a putt or a shot, I tried to lay down all the frustration and anger before going to the next hole. I am not saying I was perfect, but Lee's comment really helped. My first year I only made sixteen cuts out of thirty-five tournaments, but my second year, I made twenty-nine out of thirty-five. The difference was my attitude."

Have a good attitude about yourself. Focus your effort and concentration on the next shot. Face what lies ahead in golf, life, and faith. Forget what's past; "It's history!"

The greatest weapon any player can have is a good mental attitude.

Cracker Crenshaw
Live Each DAY; *Play Each* HOLE

*Remember, O Lord, Your tender mercies and Your
lovingkindnesses, for they are from of old.*

PSALM 25:6

Would you live any differently if today were your last day on earth? If you had only one more hole to play? Carleton "Cracker" Crenshaw had an experience that led him to ask these questions. Nicknamed for the crackers he gave to kids who lived near his dad's cookie company in Jacksonville, Florida, people loved this grand ole man's big smile, friendly manner, and deep love for Christ. Cracker played golf three or four times a week on a nine-hole navy base course near his home. One day, while playing the fourth hole, Cracker collapsed from a heart attack. Many folks were brokenhearted. His family gathered in his hospital room as he closed his eyes, apparently dead. But as they started to walk away, Cracker opened his eyes and raised up, very much alive.

From that day forward, Cracker appreciated life, seeing each day as a gift from God. He knew what it meant to have one more day with family and friends. He enjoyed each golf hole as though it were his last. He died two years later while playing the next hole, the fifth hole, on the old navy course. Ironically, Cracker had lived to play one more hole.

Appreciate each day as a gift from God. Be more expectant, grateful, and optimistic. Be a joy to others.

*Live each day;
play each hole…
as if it were your last.*

There's NO TIME
LIKE *the* PRESENT

Therefore do not worry about tomorrow,
for tomorrow will worry about its own things.

MATTHEW 6:34

Do not . . . live in the past and wonder what happened.

Do not . . . live in the future and worry about what might happen.

Instead . . . live in the present, enjoy it, and focus on what is happening now.

Take this to the golf course. Focus on the present, and play one shot at a time. Play to the best of your ability, and regardless of the outcome, remember that a bad shot is not the end of the world.

Remember the past . . .
learn from it.
Consider the future . . .
plan for it.
Live in the present . . .
enjoy it.

After many years on the Tour, Wally began thinking about what he would do with the rest of his life. He had spent twelve years on the great courses of the world, in competition with the greatest players of the sport. But his schedule kept him away from home. Playing each week with no financial guarantees made him feel uncertain about his ability to support his growing family. Burned out and insecure, Wally sought the Lord's will for his life. He wanted to know how he was to finish out his life. What would he do after playing twenty-five years of professional golf? Then Wally discovered a quote: "Life is something that happens to you while you're planning for the future." He also read Proverbs 3:5, which says to trust in the Lord with all your heart. He came to understand that he should not be anxious but should enjoy his life, trusting in the Lord every day.

STRATEGY SIX
Body, Mind, & Spirit
DISCIPLINE *Yourself to* GROW

*Therefore, my beloved brethren, be steadfast,
immovable, always abounding in the work of the Lord,
knowing that your labor is not in vain in the Lord.*

1 CORINTHIANS 15:58

This sixth strategy applies to the physical, mental, and spiritual growth we experience throughout life. As we mature through childhood, becoming bigger and stronger, we develop specific physical skills, often at high levels. It is amazing how well some young people excel in various sports—golf, tennis, basketball, gymnastics—at seemingly earlier and earlier ages. However, our physical capacity diminishes over time.

Though we may lose physical ability, there are always opportunities for mental growth. It can begin early in the home and can continue through education and training at any stage of life. Graduation from high school, college, or professional training programs completes most of our formal education. However, we need to discipline ourselves to grow mentally even after graduation.

And spiritual growth? The Holy Spirit begins to teach us as soon as we accept Jesus as Savior. Your reborn spirit is like a new seedling. Your growth is fostered by reading God's Word in the Bible, hearing the Word taught, praying to God, seeking to abide in Christ, and fellowshipping with other believers.

Growth is essential for finishing the course, so wherever you are, discipline yourself to grow—physically, mentally, and spiritually.

*Finishing the course
involves growing.*

Give a person a golf club, and
they will be frustrated every day.

Teach a person to golf, and they
will enjoy the game for a lifetime.

Betsy King
A STORY *of* DISCIPLINE

When Betsy King was inducted into the LPGA Hall of Fame, she contributed something for display that reflects her heart and her commitment to grow spiritually. It was the study Bible given to her by Captain Bill Lewis. She had carried and studied from it for almost as long as she was on the Tour. She marked meaningful passages and made notes to herself in it as she learned the Word. It is a record of her spiritual growth and a reminder of the importance of disciplining ourselves to study God's Word regularly. It is an expression of how Betsy has sought to reflect God's glory to others.

We can learn from Betsy's example as a positive role model. She has influenced many young people at Fellowship of Christian Athlete golf camps and other events. Many adults see her as a model of consistency in her walk with Christ. Betsy's commitment is also seen in her involvement in organizations like Habitat for Humanity. She, along with other golf professionals, contributes a labor of love in the building of houses throughout the world. She creates homes for those who, otherwise, would not have a place of their own.

She chose to display the dove symbol on her bag not only as a product endorsement for Dove soap but also as a sign of the peace of Christ that rules in her heart. Betsy's Bible in the LPGA Hall of Fame reminds others to study God's Word.

*I enjoy life.
When you know what
the end picture is,
it frees you up
to enjoy the present.*

BETSY KING

Jesus — *the Master* Teacher

He taught them many things by parables . . .

MARK 4:2

And so it was, when Jesus had ended these sayings,
that the people were astonished at His teaching,
for He taught them as one having authority, and not as the scribes.

MATTHEW 7:28–29

Mentally picturing yourself in a situation before it happens can help you learn. Perhaps you've found success in visualizing yourself teeing off in a tournament, giving a speech, or confronting a difficult coworker. In golf, visualizing each part of the swing and then the swing as a whole circle accelerates the learning process. For example, in the golf downswing, the right-arm motion can be compared to the underhand motion of skipping a flat rock across water.

Jesus knew that our greatest learning would come when we could visualize ourselves doing certain things or responding in a certain way. As the master storyteller, He taught people using pictures and words. Specifically, Jesus gave us the image of Himself as the shepherd, with us as His sheep. He also said, "I am the vine, you are the branches" to show that our life comes from Him (John 15:5).

The Pharisees were so wrapped up in dos and don'ts that they missed the meaning of Jesus' illustrations. To grow spiritually, we cannot focus on dos and don'ts. Instead, we need to visualize ourselves doing what we have been taught by illustration and example.

Avoid the deadly disease of "paralysis by analysis."

In Golf ... *The thing I'm proudest of is that I got better everyday.*

BEN HOGAN

In Life ... *I want to know Him a little bit better today.*

JIM SHEARD AND WALLY ARMSTRONG

Steve Jones
GROWING *through* ADVERSITY

Be strong and of good courage; do not be afraid, nor be dismayed,
for the Lord your God is with you wherever you go.
JOSHUA 1:9

Steve Jones learned to face adversity following a dirt biking accident in November 1991. The accident left Steve with several injuries. The smallest one to his left index finger kept him off the Tour for nearly three years. It appeared there was no way that he could properly hold the club, a significant adversity for a career PGA Tour golfer. He tried every sort of adjustment until, finally, he and his teacher Paul Purtzer developed an unconventional grip that worked for Steve.

When a right-handed player uses the typical overlap (or Vardon) grip, the little finger of the right hand overlaps the index finger of the left hand. The solution for Steve meant using a reverse overlap grip, similar to that used by many players for putting. He places the index finger of the left hand over the little finger of the

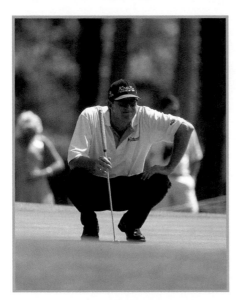

right hand. While not recommended for most players, it worked for Steve, though he had to learn to play all over again. With perseverance, discipline, and patience, however, he got back to his original form and won several tournaments, including the 1996 U.S. Open. As Steve and Tom Lehman played together in the final pairing on that day, they talked about the strength and courage found in Joshua 1:9.

God teaches us through adversity. The Lord taught Steve much about life and helped him "get a new grip" on life and golf. Those lessons have helped Steve as he later faced other health issues that impacted his play on Tour.

Be strong and courageous in the face of adversity. The Lord is with you.

The *Adjustable* Club

Some experts suggest that equipment has very little impact on score; they claim that it accounts for less than 2 percent of the variance in scores. Instead, they say that preparation, discipline, perseverance, and skill make the real difference. With this in mind, imagine an advertisement in the 1940s and 1950s that said the "Adjustable" golf club "[did] everything a set [would do]." It was an "All-in-One Golf Club" intended for "everyone interested in golf." A dial on the hozzle could be adjusted to create the loft of six different clubs: putter, driver, and three-, five-, seven-, and nine-irons. It made golf easy and thrifty.

As Christians, we are like an adjustable club. While we cannot do everything, we are called to be an instrument God can use to exercise His will on earth. We are to be faithful to His vision for us. After all, He has equipped us for the task. That is why Jesus said, "Most assuredly, I say to you, he who believes in Me, the works that I do he will do also; and greater works than these he will do, because I go to My Father" (John 14:12). This is God's promise to those who become "an adjustable club" in the hands of the Master.

Trust and adjust!

Practice *Builds* Trust

Show me Your ways, O Lord; teach me your paths.
Lead me in Your truth and teach me,
for You are the God of my salvation;
on You I wait all the day.

PSALM 25:4–5

Without the discipline of practice, you cannot face difficult shots in golf, especially under the pressure of competition. You need to go through the routine of repeatedly practicing a wide variety of shots. Practice until you can trust your ability to make each shot. Then you can face each opportunity by trusting in your preparation and abilities. Do not hesitate or overcompensate.

Professional golfers practice several hours each day because they want the necessary skills to be readily available in their mind and body. Even though he is known as "The Boss of the Moss," Loren Roberts practices putting two or three hours a day. He and the other Tour pros practice before and after a round. They build discipline into their practice. When the pressure is on and they have a particular shot to perform, they want to be ready.

Discipline enhances our faith; it helps us trust Jesus and the Bible for the answers to the challenges and opportunities of life.

God will help you
grow in faith
and knowledge
of Him.

FOCUSED PREPARATION
for GOLF *and* LIFE

- Set a goal for the round or day.
- Practice with purpose by focusing on the goal.
- Ask a coach to help you eliminate bad habits.
- Develop a preshot routine to repeat performance under pressure.
- Have fun.

Build on a
foundation of faith
by practicing the
reading and application
of God's Word
in your life.

JIM SHEARD &
WALLY ARMSTRONG
IN HIS GRIP

Service

BE A *Good Samaritan to* OTHERS

*But a certain Samaritan, as he journeyed, came to where he was.
And when he saw him, he had compassion. So he went to him
and bandaged his wounds, pouring on oil and wine; and he set him on
his own animal, brought him to an inn, and took care of him.*

LUKE 10:33

In the parable of the good Samaritan, three people pass by a man who has been stripped, beaten, and left on the road by robbers. The first is a priest; the second, a Levite. Both see him but pass by him on the other side of the road. But then the good Samaritan saw him and had compassion. All three "saw," but only the Samaritan "saw with compassion." Jesus wants us to be a good Samaritan, to see strangers and neighbors through the eyes of His compassion. Jesus sees them as the sheep of His flock, needing His help, direction, and encouragement.

A compassionate perspective requires a heart surrendered to Christ. But there is a catch: we must slow down. We must not be too busy to be compassionate. In a world that expects us to move faster and get more done in less time, we must resist the temptation to "move to the other side of the road." Instead, we must allow the heart of Christ to rule over us with the eyes, heart, and pace of a Good Samaritan.

Be a Good Samaritan to strangers and neighbors alike, such as family members, coworkers, golfing buddies, friends, and others. Those who need the compassion of Jesus are all around you, even at the golf course. Watch for them with the eyes and heart of Jesus.

*See with compassion,
and respond to the
needs of others.*

What excites me probably as much as winning is being able to make a difference in people's lives...

That's what it's all about.

PAYNE STEWART

Patty Berg
A LOVE *for* KIDS

Though she had no family of her own, Patty Berg showed her love for young people at many camps for kids conducted by Fellowship of Christian Athletes. The camps gave her the opportunity to relate to hundreds of youngsters, and she always made a sincere effort to shake hands with every one of them.

Patty gives to others out of a storehouse of love that is derived from her deep and long-lasting commitment to Jesus. It is evident Patty has been shaped by the love God has shown her. As a result, many of us love Patty as we would our own mother or grandmother. She's soft-spoken, available, and willing to listen.

Patty was also a tough competitor, a focused athlete. Over her long career, she won eighty-five tournaments, twenty-eight as an amateur and fifty-seven as a professional. Among them were fifteen major championships. She, along with Louse Suggs, Mildred "Babe" Zaharias, and Betty Jameson, was one of the original 1951 inductees to the LPGA Hall of Fame. Patty contributed to golf far beyond her performance on the course. She was one of the founders of the LPGA, and from 1949 to 1952, served as its first president.

Women's golf today owes much of its popularity to the pioneering dedication and hard work of Patty. She was an ambassador for the game at a time when the idea of a

professional golf tour for women received little, if any, popular support. Her legacy to golf is significant. Her legacy of love and commitment to others, especially kids, is eternal.

Patty Berg is the best friend the game of golf ever had; she is its Good Samaritan!

A TRUE FRIEND
is the one
who looks harder
for your lost ball
THAN YOU DO.

Show Gratitude *to* Others

Let nothing be done through selfish ambition or conceit,
but in lowliness of mind let each esteem others better than himself.
Let each of you look out not only for his own interests,
but also for the interests of others.

PHILIPPIANS 2:3–4

One way of giving to others is showing appreciation for the things they do. PGA Tour professional Bob Unger showed gratitude to people on the Tour. He went to the marshals, shook their hands, and said something like, "I appreciate your volunteering" or "You really make this tournament a blessing to the players. Thank you for contributing." He also thanked people at the transportation office for contributing cars and for driving.

You, too, have a great opportunity to encourage others by showing your gratitude and appreciation to them. You can show gratitude to others at work, restaurants, the pro shop, or the grocery store. See them as God sees them. Do you know of someone who needs a kind word, a grateful handshake, or a note of appreciation? Let your sincere gratitude be a ray of sunshine in someone's life today.

Wally expressed goodwill and thankfulness while he was on the PGA Tour. Being a Tour professional was a dream come true, and he was thankful to be there. He sent cards not only to the tournament director, but also to volunteers. He signed them, "In His Grip—Psalm 37:23–24."

You are
God's
spokesperson.

Captain Bill Lewis
SPIRITUAL FATHER *to* MANY

After retiring from the navy, Captain Bill Lewis set out to help young people find a personal relationship with Jesus Christ through the game of golf. Known to many thousands of people as Captain Bill, his vision was to make a differ-

ence. By making Jesus the captain of his own soul, Bill allowed the love of God to spill over into the lives of thousands of young people. For over twenty years, Bill worked with Fellowship of Christian Athletes to conduct golf camps around the country. Many other golf professionals and tour pros, such as Betsy King, Patty Berg, and Larry Nelson, also helped. Jack and Barb Nicklaus have sponsored a tournament that raises funds for these golf camps. When someone like Bill has a vision for helping people, others can come along and be a part of the dream.

Captain Bill has conveyed the message of what it means to live in God's grip. He tells people, "We all need the Jesus grip." When we are in His grip, we have God's infinite love and power. God is there to love us, to care for us, to touch us, and to nurture us. Most of all, kids at the camps have learned that God makes it possible for each of them to love Him back. For over thirty years, Bill Lewis has been unselfishly finishing the course. He has exposed thousands to the real Master. Like Bill, when you live your life in the hands of the Master, you will be equipped with the fruits of the Spirit, which are love, joy, peace, longsuffering, kindness, goodness, faithfulness, gentleness, and self-control (Gal. 5:22–23).

We all need
"the Jesus grip."

Bill Strausbaugh Jr.
COMMITMENT *to* PEOPLE

*Blessed be the God and Father of our Lord Jesus Christ, the Father
of mercies and God of all comfort, who comforts us in all our tribu-
lation, that we may be able to comfort those who are in any trouble,
with the comfort with which we ourselves are comforted by God.*

2 CORINTHIANS 1:3–4

Bill Strausbaugh was the PGA golf professional at the Columbia Country Club in Chevy Chase, Maryland, for twenty-seven years. In addition to being a great teacher and an ambassador for the game, he went out of his way to help others. During his first golf lesson, he would sit with a student in a gazebo to discuss his or her needs. He wanted to personalize the lessons to fit the student. Renowned for his commitment to people, the PGA of America named a national PGA award after him—the Bill Strausbaugh Club Relations Award—which is given annually to a PGA member.

When Roger Van Dyke, the golf professional at Hawk's Rest in Vero Beach, Florida, received this award, he said that it was an honor to be compared to Bill. It caused Roger to ask himself if he was the kind of person who gave to others without considering what they could do for him.

A Good Samaritan spends time with the greatest Samaritan, Jesus Christ. Choose to "go to the gazebo," or to a quiet place where you can meet with Christ each day. Then you can go out into the world to listen to people and help them.

***The key to service
is in your foundation.***

Encourage *Your* Family

Then Jethro rejoiced for all the good which the Lord had done for Israel, whom He had delivered out of the hands of the Egyptians.

EXODUS 18:9

Exodus tells the miraculous story of God's people, how Moses led them out of Egypt to the Promised Land. In the eighteenth chapter of Exodus, Moses' father-in-law, Jethro, carefully listened as Moses told about the Israelites' problems with Pharaoh, their ensuing hardships, and the Lord's gracious deliverance. After hearing the story, Jethro gave praise to God and encouraged his son-in-law (18:9).

Like Moses, we need family and friends who will listen to our successes and difficulties. We need to encourage and remind each other of God's perspective in the situation. After listening, we may offer our observations and advice.

Have you noticed how families respond to each other when they play golf? While some families have given up playing together, many families and couples enjoy their time together on the golf course. They have learned how to give and receive advice in a loving and respectful manner.

Encourage one another. Listen, observe, and comment on what God is doing. Your family deserves your best advice, delivered in a loving and caring manner.

Find ways to listen, observe, and encourage!

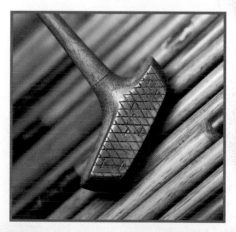

LISTENING
is a People-Oriented
PERSPECTIVE

Submit to one another out of reverence for Christ.
EPHESIANS 5:21 (NIV)

Therefore be imitators of God as dear children.
And walk in love, as Christ also has loved us
and given Himself for us, an offering and
a sacrifice to God for a sweet-smelling aroma.
EPHESIANS 5:1–2

- *Listen; really listen. Don't interrupt anyone, especially your family.*

- *Take an interest in others— especially the young, old, sick, or hurting. Use your ears to demonstrate godliness.*

- *Talk less about yourself and your accomplishments, plans, failures, or weaknesses. Don't advertise your own self-righteousness.*

- *Close your mouth so your ears can function. Let your heart "hear" the heart of others.*

- *Thank God for the people He puts in your life. Ask Him to help you listen to His perspective about them.*

Adversity

DEAL *with the* BUNKERS

My brethren, count it all joy, when you fall into various trials, knowing that the testing of your faith produces patience. But let patience have its perfect work, that you may be perfect and complete, lacking nothing.

JAMES 1:2–4

Bunkers are the many types of adversity we face on the golf course. Water, sand, trees, shrubs, and long grass are simply a part of the game. They discipline our shot making, test our skills, and make golf challenging and interesting. Similarly, the bunkers on the course of life can challenge us or can get us off track. We face sickness, tragedy, defeat, and disappointment. Though we cannot avoid difficulties in life or golf, we can learn to deal with them in the following ways.

- *Recognize there will be adversity. Accept this reality, and do not be afraid of it.*

- *Learn to avoid adversity. Though you cannot avoid every trouble,* *you can develop skills to avoid some of them. Learn skills and biblical wisdom to avoid pitfalls in life. Learn to manage the course.*

- *Learn to work through problems. Learn to hit out of the sand and difficult lies. These skills, and the right frame of mind, can improve your scores and enjoyment. In life, you can learn to get out of problem areas with the support of God and others. He will help in times of need. Remember the hope of Philippians 4:13:* I can do all things through Christ who strengthens me.

Failure is God's opportunity to help you grow.

*No matter
what happens,*

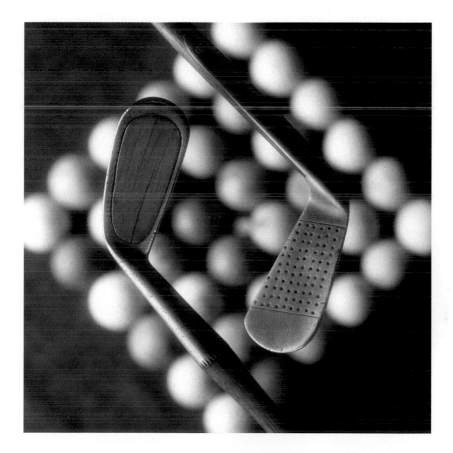

keep on hitting the ball.

HARRY VARDON

Bobby Clampett
My BIGGEST Trial

Adversity, as hard as it is, is a great teacher. Several years ago, Bobby Clampett and his wife, Ann, had to deal with the death of their newborn daughter, Sara. At the time, Bobby was struggling to earn a living on the Tour, and this tragedy brought even more pressure to bear on this young couple. Bobby and Ann chose to go forward. They learned three principles that offer good advice for dealing with adversity.

1. *Demonstrate God's power.*
2. *Prove through this ordeal that God does love me— He does care.*
3. *Demonstrate perseverance.*

Bobby learned to pray for determination and strength to make it through the tragedy.

He wrote, "[God's] allowed me to stay on the PGA this long, through all the swing changes that

I've made. He's given me a talent for a reason. I want to make the most of what I have. I pray He will use me mainly as a tool—to carry out His will and purpose." Eventually, the Clampetts had another daughter, Katelyn.

Following his career on the PGA Tour, Bobby moved on to other activities, including commentating for televised golf events. His ability to communicate in writing and in front of people not only made him successful but also gave him the opportunity to serve the Lord in many capacities.

*I only have
one goal now.
That is to
live my life
for the Lord.*

BOBBY CLAMPETT

*Trials in life have a way
of molding us into the
likeness of Christ if
we love Him first.
Difficult circumstances are
constant reminders for us
that true success begins
with the pursuit of holiness.*

BOBBY CLAMPETT
BASED ON ROMANS 8:28

Get Back *on* Track

Therefore most gladly I will rather boast in my infirmities,
that the power of Christ may rest upon me.

2 CORINTHIANS 12:9b

We seldom recognize our own fatal flaws and are often unwilling or unable to correct them on our own. Even when the problem is made clear, we find it hard to step back, change, and solve the issue. The same is true in golf. Many golfers can't understand what is wrong with their swing, but they won't go to a pro for a lesson, even when their game has fallen apart.

They haven't recognized the need, or don't want to be embarrassed. In contrast, it is interesting that Tour professionals know when they need help and seek the best coaching.

If you feel derailed in life or golf, you may need help from someone who is capable, someone who will be honest with you. This person may be a family member, a friend, or a specialist, such as a counselor, pastor, or golf professional, who can help with your "fatal flaw."

As a consultant at Personnel Decisions International, Jim helped "derailed" executives get "back on track" in their careers. Their fatal flaw, or Achilles' heel, put them in jeopardy of losing their job, but if they accepted Jim's help and learned to deal with the problem, they could usually get back on track. If not, they were likely to fail.

Recognizing
your weakness
helps you
become strong.

GOD USES FAILURE to equip us for FUTURE SUCCESS.

STEVE FARRAR

The Appeal of Golf

[Golf] offers endless problems.
It challenges our skill and
makes the accomplishment of
a difficult task a pleasure
instead of a drudgery.

JEROME D. TRAVERS AND JAMES R. CROWELL

Chi Chi Rodriguez
SHOELESS *to* SHOELESS

Chi Chi Rodriguez started life "in a bunker," with difficult odds and plenty of adversity. His father worked on a farm in Puerto Rico and raised six kids on only eighteen dollars a week. Chi Chi grew up shoeless, one of the many hardships of his poverty, but he managed to get out of his bunker and rose to the top as a very famous golfer with a big smile and an even bigger heart. He has never forgotten his roots and still identifies with the people of low position and little opportunity.

His infectious personality endears him to everyone, especially children. Chi Chi loves kids; it is evident in his smile and laughter when he's with them and in the attention he gives to them. He invests time and money in children through charities, such as his home for kids in St. Petersburg, Florida. He offers hope to those who find themselves "in the bunkers of life."

Chi Chi knows Christ is the true source of hope. He says the Lord has called him to reach out to kids, to help them deal with the adversity he faced as a young boy. While much of his time is spent at corporate golf events—with those who can afford to play golf with the rich and famous—his heart is still with kids who are less fortunate. Wherever he goes, Chi Chi offers hope. He says, "It's not how much you have or how much you make. It's how much you give back that counts."

Ours is a "shoeless to shoeless" life. Like Chi Chi, we came into the world shoeless, and we will leave shoeless, with nothing. But we can have hope and give hope to others.

God helps you
face your adversity.

Avoid *the* Traps

Do not love the world or the things in the world.

1 JOHN 2:15a

Golf course designers put traps in strategic locations to encourage great shots and to punish bad ones. Fairway traps reward playing in the fairway and greenside traps reward accurate shots to the green. Of course, some traps may actually benefit the player if they are positioned to keep an errant ball from going out of bounds, into the water, or down an incline. But you ordinarily want to avoid traps by focusing on the target. Focus on what you want to do, not on what you don't want to do. If you don't, you often end up in the very place you told yourself not to go.

We face several kinds of traps as we finish the course of life. These are the attitudes and behaviors that keep us from playing our best game because they involve a sinful, self-centered focus. Here are just a few.

- The trap of greed
- The trap of envy
- The trap of self-doubt
- The trap of self-love or pride
- The trap of _____
  (you name it)

You can avoid these traps by focusing on God's perspective. When we love and serve Him, we will love and serve others in His name. This is an outward focus on God and people rather than self.

God will help you avoid the self-centered traps of life.

Get Out *of the* Sand

Many amateur players have never learned how to get out of greenside sand traps. They may know how to move around the course, but when they are stuck in a sand trap, they usually need several strokes to get onto the green. They do not seem to realize that with just a little instruction and practice, they could improve significantly.

FIVE KEYS FOR A GREENSIDE SAND SHOT

1. Open your stance, and open the blade of your sand iron.

2. Set your feet firmly in the sand to keep yourself from slipping.

3. Focus on the sand just behind the ball, not on the ball itself.

4. Take a steep backswing; aim to hit through the sand, starting at a point that is about two inches behind the ball.

5. Swing with a smooth, powerful follow-through to a high finish. Power the club through the sand, and "spank" the ball out with the sand. The ball is moved up and out by the sand pushing behind the ball. Your club never touches the ball.

A *Sand* SAVE

We are hard-pressed on every side, yet not crushed;
we are perplexed, but not in despair;
persecuted, but not forsaken;
struck down, but not destroyed . . .

2 CORINTHIANS 4:8–9

Recovering from the sand to make par is affectionately called a "sand save." It is one of the thrills of the game. But what about the bunkers in life, the traps we get into from time to time? Many people get stuck in them. They flounder and do not ask for help. They continue in their self-centered ways and never learn to ask for help.

How do you get out of life's bunkers to experience a "sand save"? Though every problem is different, the following is a pretty solid list for most situations.

1. Acknowledge that you have a problem.

2. Listen to the counsel of wise and godly friends and counselors.

3. Read God's Word with an open heart.

4. Seek forgiveness from God and those you have hurt.

5. Forgive yourself.

6. Trust God to help push you out of the bunker and onto the green. Risk trusting His way, even though it may not be the obvious way.

The Finish

LET GO *of Your* TROPHIES

*Not that I have already attained, or am already perfected;
but I press on, that I may lay hold of that for which Christ Jesus
has also laid hold of me. . . . one thing I do, forgetting those things
which are behind and reaching forward to those things
which are behind, I press toward the goal for the prize
of the upward call of God in Christ Jesus.*

PHILIPPIANS 3:12–14

As you approach the "final hole" of your life, you want your days to count. You want to be doing God's business, not your own. You think to yourself that you should have been doing things God's way all along, but now it seems more urgent. As we let go of our trophies, we become more aware of what God wants. Earnestly seeking the eternal wreath of Christ focuses our attention on Him.

At the finish, we will face death, so we want to be certain that we are right with God. Since we cannot earn our way into heaven, we need to make sure that we are children of God. Trust your life to Him by confessing (in prayer) that Jesus is the Son of God and that He died on the cross for your sins. Only then can we can count on being in heaven with Jesus. Hallelujah!

*When you let go
of your trophies,
you will be ready
to finish the
back nine
of your life!*

What matters to God

*is His work in
the hearts of people.*

Larry Nelson
The TROPHY CASE

Larry Nelson was leading the 1981 PGA Championship going into the final round on Sunday. Because his tee time wasn't until 1:30 p.m., he could attend church, but he was distracted from the service. With a clear opportunity before him to win a major championship, he kept thinking about what it would mean for his career to win this major. He wanted to add another trophy to his case. That morning, though, he learned a very important lesson for finishing the course. The final hymn, the "Old Rugged Cross," got Larry's full attention. When he heard the words "'til my trophies at last I lay down," they spoke to his spirit. Larry realized no other trophy could mean more than the one Jesus had already earned for him on the cross. Larry also realized that when he dies, he will lay down all his golf trophies and cling to the old rugged cross that Christ endured. The pressure was lifted. He understood that nothing he could win or earn would surpass the glory of what Christ had already done for him.

Larry went out that afternoon and finished what he had started . . . and won the PGA Championship. Later, his wife gave him a framed plaque inscribed with the words of the "Old Rugged Cross"; he put it with his golf awards. Larry laid down his earthly trophies to worship the risen Savior, and he finished strong. He went on to win three majors on the PGA Tour and earned his place among the top money winners of the Senior Tour.

You can lay down your trophies and serve God. Jesus went to the old rugged cross for you.

*So I'll cherish
the Old Rugged Cross,
Till my trophies at last
I lay down;
I will cling to the
Old Rugged Cross,
And exchange it some day
for a crown.*

WORDS AND MUSIC BY
GEORGE BENNARD

Swilcan Bridge

*I am the door. If anyone enters by Me, he will be saved,
and will go in and out and find pasture.*

JOHN 10:9

The eighteenth at St. Andrews is the most famous finishing hole in golf. The fairway is wide open except for a stream angling across, and the only way to cross it is by the narrow, stone Swilcan Bridge. On the other side lies the final green and the Royal and Ancient clubhouse. Everyone who has ever played St. Andrews—"Old" Tom Morris, Sam Snead, Gary Player, Colin Montgomerie—has walked across this bridge.

The image of Arnold Palmer waving to the crowd from the Swilcan Bridge is one of the most memorable in golf. Everyone knew it would probably be the last time he crossed the bridge as a Tour golfer. In our own lives, we will someday be like Arnie, facing our last steps on the course. The Swilcan Bridge is reminiscent of John 10:9, in which Jesus says that He is the door to eternal salvation. As we cross from life into death, Jesus waits at the bridge to help us into eternal life with Him. With Him, we walk into heaven. Without Him, however, we will cross the bridge alone into eternal hell (John 14:6).

If you began a journey with Him earlier in life, He will be there at the end of the course to meet you. If you do not know Him, He is waiting for you to commit your life to Him. Even on the last hole, He welcomes you. If you join Him, He will walk with you across the bridge into eternity.

A strong finish awaits for those who lay down their trophies and accept His crown, the imperishable wreath.

*I*N THE CHRISTIAN LIFE,

it's not how you start that matters.

IT'S HOW YOU FINISH.

STEVE FARRAR

Payne Stewart
JUST *as* I AM

Payne Stewart always seemed to be his own person. When he wore his trademark knickers for the first time, he decided he kind of liked being different and then wore them at every tournament. No one else dared to infringe on his style of dress. In addition, Payne was known for his frankness and open-

ness. It was easy to quote him because he said what was on his mind. We'd all like to be just a little more that way at times, but instead, we often say what we think others expect us to say.

On the golf course, Payne's talents were obvious. He was a consistent performer, and his top game would surface when the stakes were high. He won his first U.S. Open at Hazeltine in 1991. More recently, he was the most steady and consistent performer at the 1999 U.S. Open, which was played on the very difficult Donald Ross course at Pinehurst #2. While others complained about the difficulty of the course, Payne stuck to his game plan and finished on top of the field. At the presentation of the coveted U.S. Open trophy, Payne revealed his trust in God and

appreciation to God for helping him finish strong. For Payne Stewart, this was not some hackneyed cliché. It was a revelation of his new-found faith in Christ. In his last months, Payne came to know Christ as his Savior; he was urged to do so by his children. He trusted God for the provision of his strength and for the needed balance in his life.

Some people come to this point in life early, but for others, like Payne, it is only later in life that we recognize who Christ really is and what He has done for us. Early or late, accepting Christ is the most profound event that happens to a person. It is even more profound than winning the U.S. Open at forty-two years of age as Payne did.

A Meaningful Life

Payne Stewart lived out his faith; he was generous and was committed to kids, his own and others'. He gave substantial monetary gifts to the youth of his church and to a youth club in his community. Payne stood for God in the last months of his life when he professed his faith after winning the

U.S. Open. Millions saw the photo of the bracelet his son had given him a few months earlier; the letters "WWJD?" were printed on the bracelet, which stand for "What Would Jesus Do?" Few of us will have these same opportunities to share our faith, but we will be called to give and to speak the truth in our own ways. We can only hope we will do so as admirably as Payne.

We have said you can never know when the end of life will come. Payne Stewart read and approved our description of him on the prior page just five days before his death. The airplane tragedy put his life before the world and revealed a man who had indeed "finished the course." His life example causes a person to wonder about his or her own life. We cannot redo what we have done, but we can have God's forgiveness and change our ways. We hope you, like us, are encouraged by Payne's example.

Are you living a meaningful life?

Final Thoughts
Your EPITAPH

A man wanted to leave an eternal legacy of his Savior's impact on his life, so he made sure that his tombstone was inscribed with the words "Jesus saves." The words were an everlasting witness to those who passed by his grave in southwestern Iowa. They say to all that come by, "Here is a man who knew Jesus and is now in heaven with his Father."

While epitaphs are generally messages on tombstones, it is interesting to think of what we want to say to others while we are still living. Bob Buford reminds us, "Saint Augustine said that asking yourself the question of your own legacy—What do I wish to be remembered for?—is the beginning of adulthood."

What would you put on your epitaph or tombstone?

While attending a funeral, Jim realized there were things he wanted to say to those who would gather at his own funeral. He went home and composed a message to his friends and family, expressing his love and asking forgiveness for his mistakes. Jim wrote, "If it has gone unnoticed, I want you to know I believed in God and in His Son Jesus Christ. I am sorry if I failed to show you how much God has meant to me. Trust him with your life so that you can die in peace as I have." He hoped people at his funeral would say of him, "This man was the same on the outside as he was on the inside, and on the inside, he was devoted to his Lord and Savior Jesus Christ."

What do you want people to remember about you?

What words sum up the essence of what you want your life to stand for?

Review *Your* Scorecard

Golfers typically sit down to talk after a round of golf. We toss the scorecard on the table and review our pars, birdies, and bogies. We recall three putts and sand saves. We may count our tee shots to the fairway, greens in regulation, and total putts. There may be encouragement or lighthearted kidding among the recollections. We may even discuss the newest driver, irons, or putter that could change our scores.

In this book, you have read about "the back nine of your life" and have learned nine strategies for "finishing the course." You can apply these strategies to your life today. To do this, you will need to review each of these strategies over the next few weeks. One or two friends may want to meet with you to encourage you and hold you accountable.

By yourself or with others, focus your review on one strategy at a time. Ask yourself: How am I doing? How (what) can I do better? What are my next steps in a strong finish? Which quotes or verses are meaningful in my life?

You may want to take notes and keep a journal of what God teaches you in this process. It will be like Harvey Penick's *Little Red Book* or Byron Nelson's *Little Black Book*. It will help you share your thoughts with others.

*God will
help you
shape your life
and follow through
to a great finish!*

I'VE GOT TO GIVE *thanks to the Lord*
FOR GIVING ME THE
*ability to believe
in myself.*

PAYNE STEWART

The Final Scorecard

And this is the testimony: that God has given us eternal life,
and this life is in His Son. He who has the Son has life;
he who does not have the Son of God does not have life.
These things I have written to you who believe in the name of the
Son of God, that you may know that you have eternal life,
and that you may continue to believe in the name of the Son of God.

1 JOHN 5:11–13

Most of us know that no one will ever play a perfect round of golf. But Ben Hogan, perhaps the greatest of all players, sought to play a perfect round. In fact, he had a recurring nightmare in which he played a perfect round of seventeen birdies in a row until the eighteenth hole, when he failed to birdie.

Only Christ lived a perfect life. Because He was God, He was capable of living a faultless life, one without sin. He did it for each of us. But what is the catch? The only catch is this: you must believe that He is the Son of God, He lived without sin, and He gave His life as the price for your sins (1 John 1:8–9; John 3:15–18). That is what it means to believe, to be "born again," to have faith, to be a Christian, and to be a follower of Christ (John 3:3–8).

If you deny Jesus, you will present your own scorecard to God. And you know it will not be perfect. If you believe in Christ, His perfect scorecard will replace your own. He "played the perfect round" for you by giving His life for you. His perfect score has been "attested" by God.

Have you accepted
Christ's perfect scorecard
for your life?

SEEKING *Perfection*

Not that I have already attained,
or am already perfected . . .

PHILIPPIANS 3:12

Golfers can identify with Philippians 3:12. Bob Rotella's book, *Golf is Not a Game of Perfect*, confirms that perfection is impossible, but we can still strive to play well. The following questions, derived from Philippians 3:12–14, can serve to challenge each of us.

- *Do you press on in your life of faith in Jesus Christ?*

- *Do you forget what lies behind? Or do you worry and feel guilty about the past?*

- *Do you push forward to what lies ahead? Do you serve Him with faith?*

- *Are you mature, or maturing, in your faith so that you hold onto what you know is true?*

- *Do you allow God to reveal to you that which is, and is not, of Him?*

To "press on," to seek after the upward call, is to strive toward unreachable perfection, knowing that Jesus will be there to help in the quest. With Jesus, we can place our trust in God. Jesus gave His perfect life so that God could see us without blemish.

We are
made perfect
in the sight
of God.

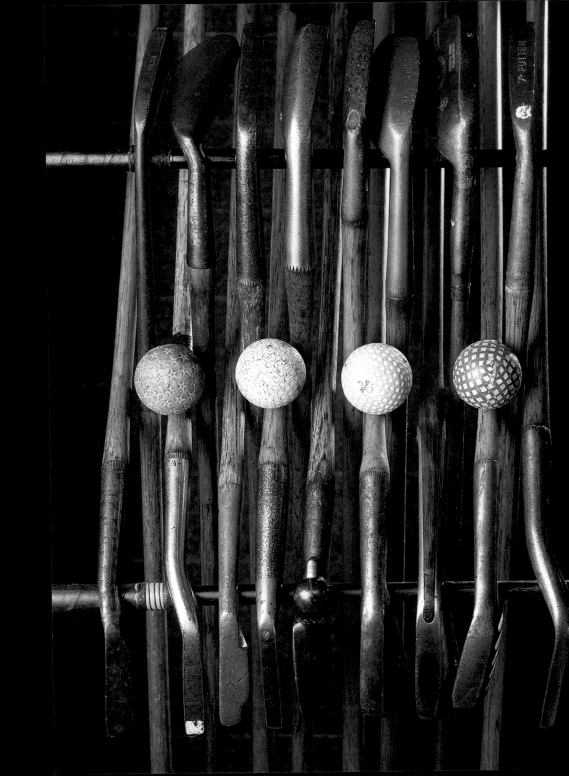

Acknowledgements

Grateful acknowledgement is made to the following:

Achenbach, Jerry. 1997. *The LINKS Letter.* Vol. 17, No. 2.

Armour, Tommy. 1953. *How to Play Your Best Golf All the Time.* New York: Simon and Schuster.

Bell, Peggy Kirk. 1999. *Golf.* May/June.

Bolt, Tommy. 1999. *The Hole Truth.* Antium Heights Publishing.

Buford, Bob. 1994. *Half Time: Changing Your Game Plan from Success to Significance.* Grand Rapids, MI: Zondervan.

Carlson, Richard. 1997. *Don't Sweat the Small Stuff . . . and it's all small stuff.* New York: Hyperion.

Clampett, Bobby. 1988. *The LINKS Letter.* Vol. 8, No. 3.

Farrar, Steve. 1995. *Finishing Strong.* Sisters, OR: Multnomah Books.

Flory, Tom. 1997. *The LINKS Letter.* Vol. 17, No. 2.

Hogan, William Ben. Original document source unknown.

Jones, Steve. Quoted in Darden, Robert, and Richardson, P. J. 1996. *The Way of an Eagle.* Nashville: Thomas Nelson Publishers.

Kelfer, Russell. Cassette message. San Antonio, TX: Discipleship Tape Ministries, 1970s.

Kemper, Jim. 1985. *The LINKS Letter.* Vol. 2, No. 3.

Langer, Bernhard. *The LINKS Letter.*

Lucado, Max. Quoted in Darden, Robert, and Richardson, P. J. 1996. *The Way of an Eagle.* Nashville: Thomas Nelson Publishers.

Massengale, Rik. *The LINKS Letter.*

Morley, Pat. Notes taken by Wally Armstrong in a Bible study with Pat Morley.

Nelson, Byron. 1995. *The Little Black Book.* Arlington, TX: Summit Publishing Group, xiii. 817-588-3013.

Nicklaus, Jack, with Ken Bowden. 1974. *Golf My Way.* New York: Simon and Schuster.

Palmer, Arnold. 1994. *Arnold Palmer— Personal Journey.* Thomas Houser, Collins Publishing.

Penick, Harvey, with Bud Shrake. 1992. *Harvey Penick's Little Red Book: Lessons and Teachings from a Lifetime in Golf.* New York: Simon and Schuster.

Prain, E. M. with Wally Armstrong and Tom Lehman. 1994. *Live Hands.* South Laguna, CA: Sports Log Publishers.

Rodriguez, Chi Chi. 1992. "Golf's Man on the Move, Chi A-Go-Go, Reflects on the Journey," by Tim Rosoforte. *Golf Illustrated.* April.

Rogers, Bill. *The LINKS Letter.*

Rotella, Bob, with Bob Cullen. 1995. *Golf Is Not a Game of Perfect.* New York: Simon and Schuster.

Sheard, Jim, and Wally Armstrong. 1997. *In His Grip: Foundations for Life and Golf.* Nashville: J. Countryman.

Simpson, Scott. Quoted in Darden, Robert, and Richardson, P. J. 1996. *The Way of an Eagle.* Nashville: Thomas Nelson Publishers, 214.

Travers, Jerome D., and James R. Crowell. 1926. *The Fifth Estate.* New York: Knopf, 139-140.

Vardon, Harry. 1966. Quoted in *Bobby Jones on Golf,* by Robert Tyre (Bobby) Jones. Garden City, NY: Doubleday, 4.

JIM SHEARD *and*
WALLY ARMSTRONG

JIM SHEARD has a Ph.D. in organizational behavior and was an executive and consultant for more than twenty-five years. Since retiring from business, he has devoted his time to writing and speaking. He has been an avid amateur golfer and a serious student of the game for most of the past fifteen years. This is Jim's third book on golf, life, and faith; with Wally Armstrong, he coauthored two previous best-sellers, *In His Grip* and *Playing the Game*. Jim is also the coauthor of *A Champion's Heart*, a book devoted to a wide variety of sports.

WALLY ARMSTRONG competed in over three hundred PGA Tour events worldwide, gaining a lifetime PGA membership. In his first Masters tournament, Wally finished just three strokes behind Gary Player, setting a record rookie score of 280. Since retiring from the Tour, he has become a renowned golf teacher. He is well-known for his

clinics on the golf swing. While serving as a caddie for legendary players like Gary Player, Wally heard Billy Graham use analogies from golf to teach spiritual truths from the Bible. Wally has put that knowledge to use in his own videos, clinics, and books on golf.

Jim and Wally share a common desire to encourage others in the game of golf and, more importantly, in life. Their unique approach to the tough issues of life, as found in their books and other materials, has made a life-changing impact on numerous individuals. Many people have continued to learn through small group studies that use their books.

Please contact us for more information on:

- *Ordering study guides for these books*
- *Starting a golf fellowship*
- *Hosting a golf event*
- *Other resources for golfers on life and faith*

In His Grip Resources
P.O. Box 642
Owatonna, MN 55060-0642
1-507-455-3377
1-888-899-GRIP (4747)
www.in-his-grip.com

P.S.

We believe Payne Stewart's life exemplifies what we have been writing about. As the stories emerged about his commitment of faith in Christ, and as we began to understand the kind of man he was seeking to become, we realized that Payne successfully finished the course—he received his crown. The stories about Payne's life and death, including those told by his friends and wife at his memorial service, illustrate how we are to finish the course. In this way, Payne taught us these important lessons.

- *Learn to laugh and cry.*
- *Reach out to others every day.*
- *Spend time with your kids.*
- *Tell your wife or husband you love them . . . every day.*
- *Find something you love doing and do it.*
- *Let Christ rule your heart.*
- *Give to others out of the richness of your blessings.*
- *Call your mom or dad often.*

- *Learn to ask what is enough, because you probably already have it.*
- *Learn that defeat is an opportunity to learn on the way to success.*
- *Remember that your friends are one of the greatest riches God will give you.*

Payne's public and personal life barely differed. People loved him, and he loved them back. We, like many of you, feel a deep sense of loss in his tragic and untimely death. Hopefully, each of us has learned from Payne, from his life and death. Perhaps his example will help you as you finish the back nine of your life.

JIM AND WALLY